BOATS

BOATS

BY KEN ROBBINS

SCHOLASTIC INC.
NEW YORK

PATRICIA MORAN

For Jimmy Salant

Many thanks are due to Brenda Bowen, whose idea this book originally was; to Tim Gleason and Doug Kuntz, who generously trusted me with their negatives; and to Sheila Buff, for all her patience and help with photo research.

Copyright © 1989 by Ken Robbins.

Library of Congress Cataloging-in-Publication Data

Robbins, Ken.
  Boats.

  Summary: Describes in text and photographs the characteristic features of seventeen different ships and boats, including tugboats, submarines, fishing boats and icebreakers.
  1. Ships—Juvenile literature. 2. Boats and boating—Juvenile literature. [1. Ships. 2. Boats and boating]
I. Title.
VM150.R6 1989   387.2   88-18329
ISBN 0-590-41157-8

12 11 10 9 8 7 6 5 4 3 2 1   9/8 0 1 2 3 4/9

Printed in the U.S.A.   36

First Scholastic printing, September 1989

Designed by Edward Miller

Look out over the ocean, or any lake, river, or harbor near your home. You'll probably see at least one boat. Because wherever there's a large body of water, there will be boats.

People have traveled on water ever since someone first climbed on a floating log to cross a river. From this early beginning, boats have been designed to help people do what they want — whether it's to cross an ocean, earn a living, explore the unknown, or spend a quiet afternoon enjoying the water.

Canoe

The canoe was one of the first types of boats ever built. Canoes still look like the ones American Indians built long ago out of wood and bark. Long and narrow, they can only hold a few people and are light enough to carry. Since they tip over very easily, they are used in calm waters. Canoeists use paddles to glide quietly through the water.

Rowboat

A rowboat is another small boat. Rowers sit facing backwards and pull on a set of oars to make the boat go forward. Rowboats are great to fish from or to travel short distances.

Racing Shell

A racing shell is a kind of rowboat that is built for speed. It is long, light, and narrow, and is rowed with special oars that are curved at the bottom, called sculls. Some people row racing shells for exercise, but mostly they are used for racing other boats. Some shells are very long and hold up to eight rowers.

Sailboat

Sailboats come in many sizes and shapes, but they all have one thing in common: They rely on the power of the wind to travel through the water. Most sailboats have a mast to hold the sails and a rudder, like a movable fin, that helps steer the boat.

Tall Ship

Until the 1800s, most great seafaring ships were wind driven. These ships had at least three masts to hold their many sails. Now only a few hundred of those old sailing vessels are left. Some can be visited at special seaport museums; others are used to train new sailors.

Motorboat

Motorboats have engines to move them, rather than paddles, oars, or the wind. The engine turns a propeller, which pushes the boat through the water. Some motorboats can zip across the water at speeds of up to 90 miles per hour and are built especially for racing. But most motorboats are used just for fun — for fishing, waterskiing, or simply relaxing.

Yacht

Although most people think of yachts as fancy and expensive, they don't have to be. Yachts are boats used for pleasure. They come in all sizes, from small ones to very large ones. There are motor yachts and sailing yachts and some that have both engines and sails. Motor yachts with small cabins on them to provide shelter are called cabin cruisers.

Houseboat

Houseboats are boats people live in, like mobile homes. They have kitchens, bedrooms, living rooms, and even telephones and electricity. Houseboats are usually kept tied up at a dock, but when their owners want to move somewhere else, they simply cast off the ropes and float away.

Ferryboat

Ferryboats are working boats. They carry people back and forth across the water from one place to another. Some are small and carry just a few people and a few cars; others are almost as big as passenger liners.

Tugboat

Tugboats are used to help huge ships, like tankers and freighters, get in and out of a harbor. They also rescue ships in trouble or tow other boats. Tugboats must have very strong engines, since they are often pulling or pushing boats much bigger than they are.

Fishing Boat

A fishing boat is another kind of working boat. The boat pulls a large net behind it through the water. When the net is full of fish, powerful engines slowly draw it onto the deck. The fish are then emptied into storage compartments and brought back to shore to be sold.

Icebreaker

The icebreaker is also a working boat. Its bow is rounded and unusually strong and heavy. When water freezes, it's the icebreaker's job to help other boats get through by smashing and pushing ice away.

Freighter

A freighter is a ship that carries cargo. The cargo could be anything from bananas to video games, from sneakers to chocolates. Freighters store cargo on their decks and below in their holds. Modern freighters, called containerships, are designed so that tractor trailers full of cargo can be lifted directly on and off the ship.

Tanker

Tankers also carry cargo, but their cargo is liquid. Very often it's oil, but it could be something else, like liquid chemicals. The holds of tankers are filled up or emptied by pumps when the ship is in harbor. The biggest tanker in the world holds up to 150 million gallons.

Liner

Because a passenger liner carries people, most of the space on these very large ships is divided into cabins where travelers stay while on board. Before there were jets, the most common way to travel across the sea was by liner. Most liners are now used as cruise ships. The largest liners carry nearly 2,000 people.

Aircraft Carrier

An aircraft carrier is like an airport floating in the ocean.
Navy aircraft take off and land on the big flat top of the
ship. Planes are stored below. Pilots, mechanics, and sailors
all live on the ship. Together there may be almost 6,000
people on board a large carrier — as many as in a
whole town.

Submarine

Submarines are the only boats designed to operate underwater. While some submarines are used to explore the ocean depths, most carry missiles and torpedos in case of war. The first submarine helped the Union forces win the Civil War. The nuclear-powered submarines of today can stay underwater for more than two months at a time.

The Parts of a Boat

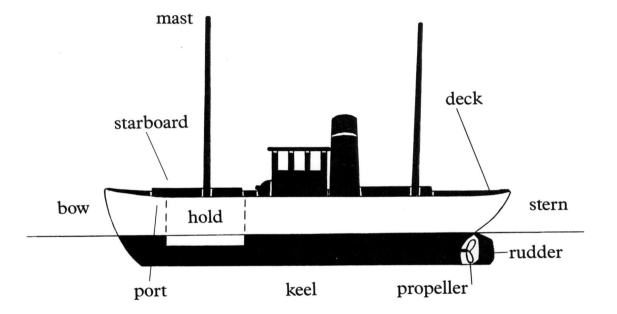

mast

starboard

deck

bow

hold

stern

port

keel

propeller

rudder